PRAISE FOR *JESUS: GOD AMONG US*

In Roger Hutchison's new book, *Jesus: God Among Us,* he reminds us that "a small child will lead [us]. It may involve a long and winding journey, but with cross held high, we will soon find our way home."

In this moment in history, we are all on a journey. For many, it may seem to be a journey of despair, of going nowhere, or worse, going backward to Egypt and enslavement. But in Roger's book, through Holy Scripture, visual art, and personal reflection, we are invited to remember that it is Jesus who is guiding us along the true and joyful journey. I have known Roger as a visual artist. In this new book, however, I have discovered he is also a dancer—moving effortlessly from Word to words, from image to reflection, and back again. It is not a solitary dance we are shown, but rather we are invited to join in the dance, to consider our own responses to Word and words, image and reflection.

This is a book for this time, a timeless reminder that the Incarnation continues to enliven our lives and our time. We are on a journey. *Jesus: God Among Us,* reminds us that the journey, while it may be long and winding, will lead all of us home, to the Incarnate God who is already in us and calling us again.

—*The Rt. Rev. Brian L. Cole, 5th Bishop of the Diocese of East Tennessee*

Roger's book *Jesus: God Among Us,* is a provocation of hope. The bold suggestive images combined with questions for reflection invite all of us to imagine; that we can let God's imagination flow through each of us in art, words, and actions. What a wonderful way to pray; to pray in hope.

—*Jamie Coats, Director of the Friends of the Society of St. John the Evangelist*

Part devotional, part study, and all heart, Hutchison's book *Jesus: God Among Us* engages the senses and the soul to discover the meaning of Christianity both in Jesus' time and in our modern world.

Relatable and starkly poignant, this book is beautiful in its simplicity. From calling into question the belongingness of refugees to sharing simple experiences from church on Sunday morning, Hutchison's work will invite, inspire, and stir both the imagination and moral center of all who encounter it. Intergenerational, holistic, and warm, this book will welcome and challenge modern Christians and seekers alike to encounter the Jesus that was, and still is.

With language simple enough to invite readers of any age but connections complex enough to stir the most seasoned souls, *Jesus: God Among Us,* is a treasure for all.

—*Emily Ainsworth Keniston, Christian educator*

Roger Hutchison creates sacred, breathtaking art out of ordinary images like dishwater and fingernail polish. His reflection questions invite deep contemplation. I will pray my way through this collection again.

—*The Rev. Elizabeth Felicetti, Rector, St. David's Episcopal Church in Richmond, Virginia*

Roger Hutchison's beautiful book uses both words and images to paint a moving portrait of Jesus. He draws on the Gospel story—just as alive then as now—and invites the reader into the creative process by asking us where we see Jesus in our own life. In a grandmother's love? A child's innocence? The mirror? At its heart, Hutchison's book is an invitation for us to live the story and reflect the image of *Jesus: God Among Us.*

—*Paige Britt, best-selling children's author of* Why Am I Me?

ROGER HUTCHISON

JESUS

GOD AMONG US

Church Publishing
NEW YORK

Church Publishing
19 East 34th Street
New York, NY 10016
www.churchpublishing.org

Cover art: *The Life of Christ* by Roger Hutchison
Design and layout by Paul Soupiset

Library of Congress Cataloging-in-Publication Data

Names: Hutchison, Roger, author.
Title: Jesus : God among us / Roger Hutchison.
Description: New York : Church Publishing, 2018.
Identifiers: LCCN 2017040103 (print) | LCCN 2017046529 (ebook) | ISBN
   9781640650022 (ebook) | ISBN 9781640650015 (pbk.)
Subjects: LCSH: Jesus Christ—Biography. | Jesus Christ—Art.
Classification: LCC BT301.3 (ebook) | LCC BT301.3 .H88 2018 (print) | DDC
   232—dc23
LC record available at https://lccn.loc.gov/2017040103

to

You ...
The healers
The creators
The lovers
+
The peacemakers.

"Little children, I am with you only a little longer.
You will look for me; and as I said to the Jews so
now I say to you, 'Where I am going, you cannot
come.' I give you a new commandment, that you
love one another. Just as I have loved you, you
also should love one another. By this everyone
will know that you are my disciples, if you have
love for one another."

—John 13:33–35

CONTENTS

FOREWORD

There is a familiar tale of a kindergarten student hard at work with her crayons and a piece of paper after her teacher asked the students to draw a picture of someone they love. As the teacher walked up and peeked at her work, she asked the girl whose image she was drawing. Without stopping her work, the girl answered with one word: "God." Trying not to let her amusement be too obvious, the teacher gently reminded her, "But no one knows what God looks like." Looking up, the girl replied, "They will when I'm done."

Thankfully, we do have a very good picture of what God looks like. Just look at Jesus. As it says in the New Testament, in the Epistle to the Colossians (1:15), Jesus "is the image of the invisible God," so if we want to know what God looks like, we can begin with "the Word become flesh," Jesus. And if we want to show the world around us what God looks like, then we must reflect in our own lives the same loving, liberating, and life-giving way that we see in Jesus as revealed throughout the Gospels.

Roger Hutchison's book, *Jesus: God Among Us,* offers all who would be part of the movement Jesus inaugurated—as well as any who are simply curious and want to know more about who this Jesus is—a wonderful glimpse into the Gospels. Hutchison takes a moving piece of personal artwork and breaks it down into pieces to serve as the lenses through which to view various biblical stories of Jesus. But he doesn't stop there, as we also find reflections both inspiring and challenging to our own world and our own situations.

Do you want to know Jesus better? Do you want to follow the way of Jesus more closely in your own life? Do you want to give your life more fully to the way, the cause, the Jesus Movement in our world today? Then Roger Hutchison's new book (a worthy successor to his earlier work, *Under the Fig Tree: Poems and Images for Lent*) is well worth reading, marking, learning, and inwardly digesting.

The Most Reverend Michael Bruce Curry

INTRODUCTION

Jesus: God Among Us is my attempt at sharing with you the sometimes pivotal, oftentimes ordinary, moments where I've glimpsed Jesus's face or experienced his presence firsthand.

Jesus isn't just what was. Jesus is here now.

You don't have to look very far to see that our world is in crisis. Racism, violence, injustice, inequity, bigotry, and hatred—these are the headlines. For many it is the reality they are faced with every day.

It seems to be getting worse.

Being an artist and writer, I believe that both word and art carry incredible power.

So I got to work.

I read my Bible, painted with my fingers, and wrote down the words that you now hold in your hand.

Please join me for this personal and hope-filled journey.

Our world is in crisis, but you don't have to look very far to see that the "love that passes all understanding" is with us now and will never leave us.

This is a love that can right the ship in the midst of any storm.

This love is Jesus.

God among us.

Roger Hutchison
Houston, Texas
June 15, 2017

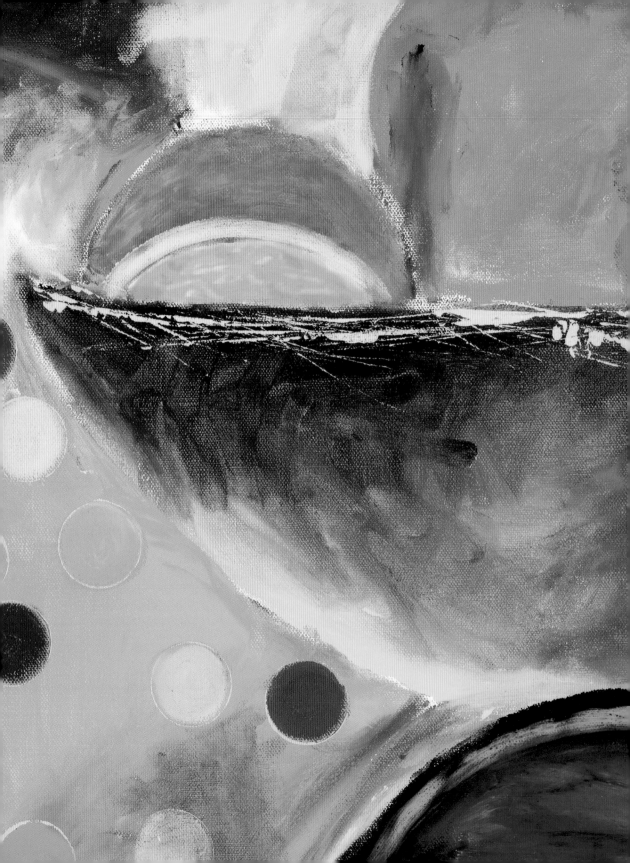

I. NO PLACE

In those days a decree
went out from Emperor
Augustus that all
the world should be
registered. This was
the first registration
and was taken while
Quirinius was governor
of Syria. All went to
their own towns to
be registered. Joseph
also went from the
town of Nazareth in
Galilee to Judea, to
the city of David called
Bethlehem, because he
was descended from
the house and family of
David. He went to be
registered with Mary,
to whom he was
engaged and who was
expecting a child. While
they were there, the
time came for her to
deliver her child.
And she gave birth
to her firstborn son
and wrapped him
in bands of cloth
and laid him in
a manger, because
there was no place
for them in the inn.

LUKE 2:1-7

THEN

She was tired, yes, but strong, determined, and brave.

She gave birth to her son surrounded
by curious barn animals and laid him in a manger.
Joseph stayed with her, keeping watch throughout the night.

No place. No room for them in the inn.
No midwife or nurse to clean and
care for her and the baby.

Fear could have overwhelmed; anticipation,
joy, and awe kept dread at bay.

There may have been no place for them in the inn
or in Nazareth, but with the birth of their son,
they found their place ... on the run,
in a barn, cradling their new son ...

The young child cried out in the night.

Love incarnate pulled closely
for mother's milk and warmth.

NOW

It was time for her baby to be born.

She was excited and scared to death.

She was prepared but not ready.

She and her husband were on the run; strangers in a
new country with no place to call home. With the little
money they had, they were able to find a basic hotel room.
Through the generosity of the manager, they were able to
have enough to eat and felt safe—most of the time.

Her water broke and she knew it was time.
Her husband ran to get help.

Her husband put his arm around her and walked her to the
stranger's car. The kind stranger rushed them to the local
hospital, where soon after their daughter was born.

The newborn cried out in the night and they
knew their lives would never be the same.

The young mother cradled her daughter close, said a
prayer, and quietly sang a lullaby—the same lullaby her
mother sang to her many moons and miles ago.

FOR REFLECTION

Have you ever experienced
a "No Place"?

Where do you find safety?

II. LOST & FOUND

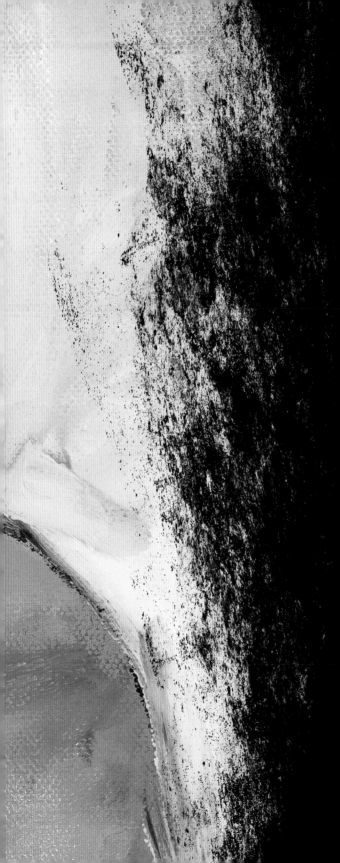

Now every year his parents went
to Jerusalem for the festival of the
Passover. And when he was twelve
years old, they went up as usual for the
festival. When the festival was ended
and they started to return, the boy
Jesus stayed behind in Jerusalem, but his
parents did not know it. Assuming that
he was in the group of travelers, they
went a day's journey. Then they started
to look for him among their relatives
and friends. When they did not find him,
they returned to Jerusalem to search
for him. After three days they found
him in the temple, sitting among the
teachers, listening to them and asking
them questions. And all who heard him
were amazed at his understanding and
his answers. When his parents saw him
they were astonished; and his mother
said to him, "Child, why have you
treated us like this? Look, your father
and I have been searching for you in
great anxiety." He said to them, "Why
were you searching for me? Did you
not know that I must be in my Father's
house?" But they did not understand
what he said to them. Then he went
down with them and came to Nazareth,
and was obedient to them. His mother
treasured all these things in her heart.

And Jesus increased in wisdom and in
years, and in divine and human favor.

LUKE 2:41–52

THEN

Children love to play and wander;
Jesus was no different.

His parents had told him over
and over to stay close.

Mary chuckled when Jesus ran off
to play with the other children.

"That boy is something else," she said to
herself. "I hope he doesn't get lost."

After the festival of the Passover had ended and they had traveled for a full day, Mary and Joseph started looking for Jesus.

They checked with his friends. They had not seen him since they had been in Jerusalem. In fact, they weren't sure he had left Jerusalem. Mary began to worry— frantically searching for Jesus in the crowd of travelers.

Joseph and Mary turned around and headed back to Jerusalem. Their son was missing and they had to find him.

"Jesus! Where are you?" Mary cried out along the way.

For three long days and nights, they searched for their son.

On the third day, they found Jesus in the temple.

He wasn't playing or causing trouble.

He was listening to the teachers and asking them questions—questions that stunned those who were gathered around. "Child! What in the world are you doing? We have been looking for you for three days! Why did you do this?" Mary was on the verge of tears. Anger and relief boiled in her heart.

There was also a sense of curious knowing that began to take shape in Mary's heart.

"Why were you searching for me?" Jesus asked, incredulously. "Did you not know I would be in my Father's house?"

Mary, Joseph, and Jesus returned to Nazareth.

The following years were good ones. Jesus was a hardworking and obedient young man. He loved to study and seemed destined for something special.

Mary would never forget the time that Jesus was lost, then found.

NOW

Each Sunday, following the singing of the Psalm, the children leave their parents and join me behind a small processional cross for what we call "Liturgy Preparation." The children are led out of church behind the children's cross during the gospel hymn and return at the exchange of the Peace.

During our time together, the children have the opportunity to worship and learn about the gospel lesson for the day. It is a holy time of singing together, praying together, and exploring a story about Jesus.

I am always surprised by how excited the children get when they get to carry the cross. They take it in their small hands and with great aplomb; they lift the cross into the air and lead the rest of the children down the aisle and out of the nave of the church. An adult or teenager often brings up the end of the line.

We don't want to lose anyone.

I am the one who is supposed to teach the children each week; each week the children are the ones who teach me. They are eager and hungry to learn and love to share with me the miracles they see every day.

We, as adults, can learn a great deal from the children in our midst. We just have to pay attention.

When it is time to return, the cross is lifted high into the air and carried back into the nave.

I watch—and hold my breath each week as the children return to their parents.

Without fail, there is always the wanderer or daydreamer that takes forever to find his parents. The child goes one way and the parents go the other.

Then, finally small hand finds big hands and everyone is back where he or she belongs.

Then, I am able to breathe.

A small child will lead them. It may involve a long and winding journey, but with cross held high, we will soon find our way home.

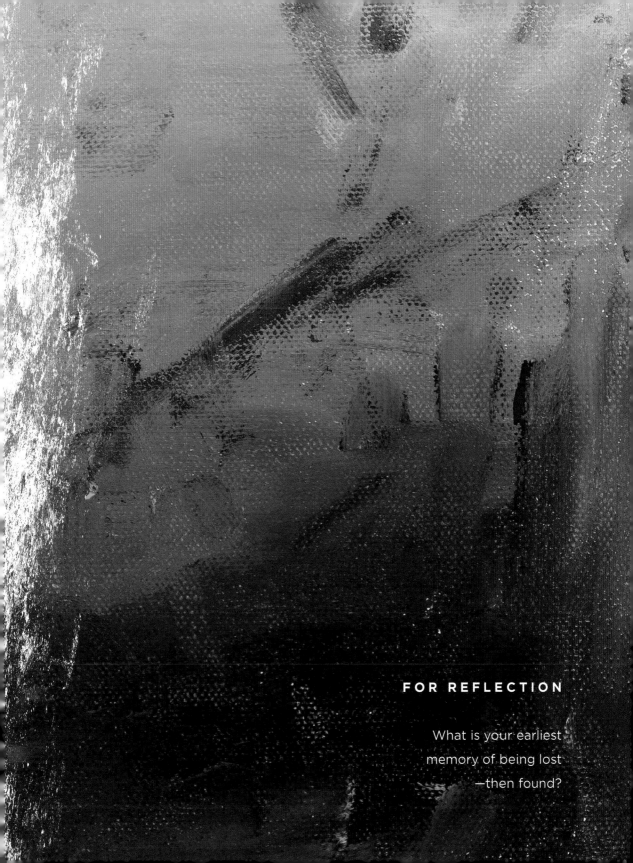

FOR REFLECTION

What is your earliest
memory of being lost
—then found?

III. THE HEAVENS WERE OPENED

Then Jesus came from Galilee to John at the Jordan, to be baptized by him. John would have prevented him, saying, "I need to be baptized by you, and do you come to me?" But Jesus answered him, "Let it be so now; for it is proper for us in this way to fulfill all righteousness." Then he consented. And when Jesus had been baptized, just as he came up from the water, suddenly the heavens were opened to him and he saw the Spirit of God descending like a dove and alighting on him. And a voice from heaven said, "This is my Son, the Beloved, with whom I am well pleased."

MATTHEW 3:13–17

THEN

The "voice who cries out."

A Jewish itinerant preacher, John roamed the wilderness heralding the arrival of the Messiah.

Clothed in camel's hair and leather, John was filled with the Spirit of God. His appearance and demeanor were reminiscent of prophets of old— especially Elijah. He was called demonic. Crazy, even.

His sustenance came from a diet of locusts and wild honey.

The people loved him and followed him with intense fervor, for his biting message of the impending arrival of "God in the flesh" was an intriguing and powerful one.

Corruption ran deep among the people and John told them that they must repent, "for the kingdom of heaven is at hand."

Then, Jesus was there—in the water with the Baptizer.

Not one to hold back, John said to Jesus, "You want me to baptize you? I'm the one that needs you to baptize me."

Jesus commanded John to baptize him.

John took Jesus in his arms and submerged him into the River Jordan. The crowds had gathered to watch. The air was electric.

When Jesus came up from the water, the heavens opened, and God appeared in the form of a dove. John knew in the depths of his heart and soul that the Messiah had arrived.

"This is my son, the Beloved."

NOW

It is late afternoon in France under a crisp blue sky. I am covered from head
to toe in water and soap bubbles, a volunteer in the open-air kitchen. The
sea of voices around me rises up like a symphony, instruments that I do not
recognize, yet long to understand and know. I hear sounds of laughter and joy.

So much unrestrained laughter and joy . . .

There are faces that I recognize. I see a young woman and a young
man who traveled with me to Taíze: Tom saw God's face clearly for
the first time as he looked into the painted face of the crucified
Jesus icon in the community church. Hillary feels in her heart that
she will never be the same person she was before this journey.

She, too, saw God's face.

Then, there are faces that I do not know, but have seen before.

When I was young, I used to pore over my grandmother's copies of
National Geographic magazine. I would look for hours at the pictures
of the black—nearly blue-black—faces of strikingly beautiful African
men and women. As I gaze across the way, I see her again. It is as if
the picture in the magazine has come to life. That beautiful black
face. Those dark and deep eyes. That bright encompassing smile.

Then I glance across to the faces of
my new friends Adrian and Olgutsa.
A boyfriend and girlfriend who traveled
to this small village from Romania
are also seeking the face of God.

They, too, communicate
with laughter, broken
English, and their eyes.
These children of God are
communicating with each other
across water; no longer separated
by the water of the ocean,
we communicate over a
basin of dishwater.

This is baptism, a more honest
and sincere form of conversation
than I have ever experienced.

It is not with our voices, for we
speak different languages. It
is with our eyes and it is with
our laughter. We are speaking
the language of the heart.

And we are washing dishes.

I look down into the basin of
dishwater and at the reflection
of the faces of my new friends.
The dancing water and the
shifting light have caused
our faces to become one.

I, too, have discovered
the face of Christ.

"This is my Beloved."

**FOR
REFLECTION**

Have you ever seen
the face of Christ?
If so, describe it using
words or images.

IV. FISH FOR PEOPLE

As he walked by the Sea of Galilee, he saw two brothers, Simon, who is called Peter, and Andrew his brother, casting a net into the sea—for they were fishermen. And he said to them, "Follow me, and I will make you fish for people." Immediately they left their nets and followed him. As he went from there, he saw two other brothers, James son of Zebedee and his brother John, in the boat with their father Zebedee, mending their nets, and he called them. Immediately they left the boat and their father, and followed him.

MATTHEW 4:18–22

THEN

"Follow me, and I will make you fish for people."

Simon, who is called Peter, and Andrew his
brother were fisherman and they had just
cast their net into the Sea of Galilee.

He called them by name.

Immediately—without question or
delay—they went with him.

The motley crew continued their journey
alongside the water's edge.

Two more brothers are called by name.

"James and John: follow me."

Immediately.

Without delay or hesitation they left
their father and their boat.

Immediately.

They followed him.

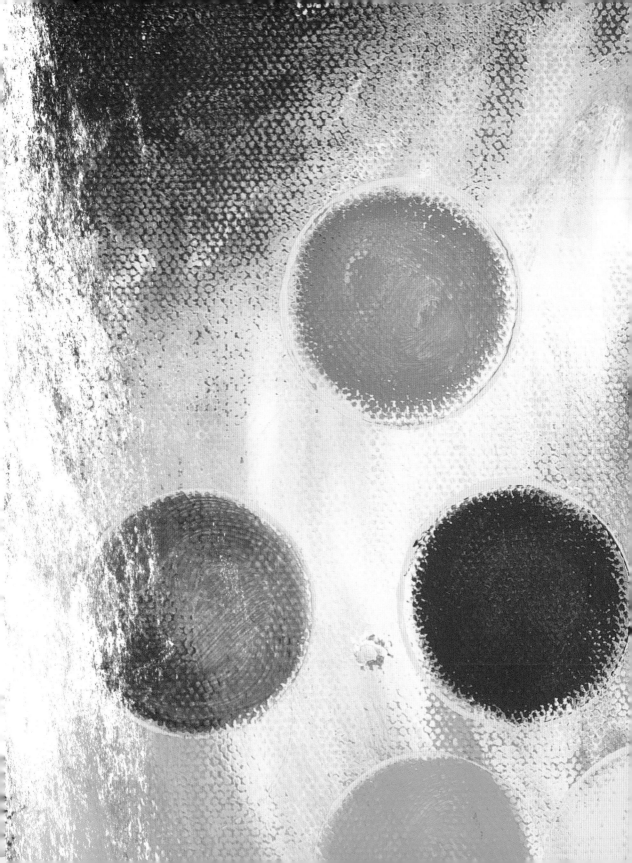

NOW

My Mammaw and I shared a love of fishing.

One of the things we enjoyed doing together was taking off through the woods down to Goodson Creek. We would find "the spot" and put our cane poles into the murky creek water. Within moments, the bobber would begin to twitch and dance around, then quickly disappear. There is nothing like catching a slimy mud catfish or a colorful sun perch on a cane pole. I would get so excited with each and every catch—and Mammaw would giggle at me with such joy and glee.

To get to our favorite fishing spot, we had to cross a cow pasture. Key word: cow. You see, I am afraid of cows. Not so much anymore, but when I was younger, I was terrified of any member of the bovine community.

One day, as we were crossing the valley of shadow and death—the pasture, a giant cow appeared out of nowhere and started walking toward us. I was probably thirteen or fourteen years old and a big boy. My Mammaw kept walking straight ahead—head held tall with no fear. Petrified, I started groaning and sidestepping to be closer to her.

I needed her to protect me from the cow!

My Mammaw picked up a small stick and shooed the creature away. What a sight we had to be—a little old lady with a small stick in one hand, and the hand of her big ole wimpy grandson in the other.

Amazingly, the cow stopped and just watched us as we disappeared into the woods. Now talk about a story that made her giggle!

Jesus said, "Follow me, and I will make you fish for people."

Immediately they left the boat and followed him.

My Mammaw took my hand and said, "Come with me. I will keep you safe." And she did.

Have you experienced Jesus's
call to follow him?
How have you answered that call?

V. GREAT CROWDS FOLLOWED HIM

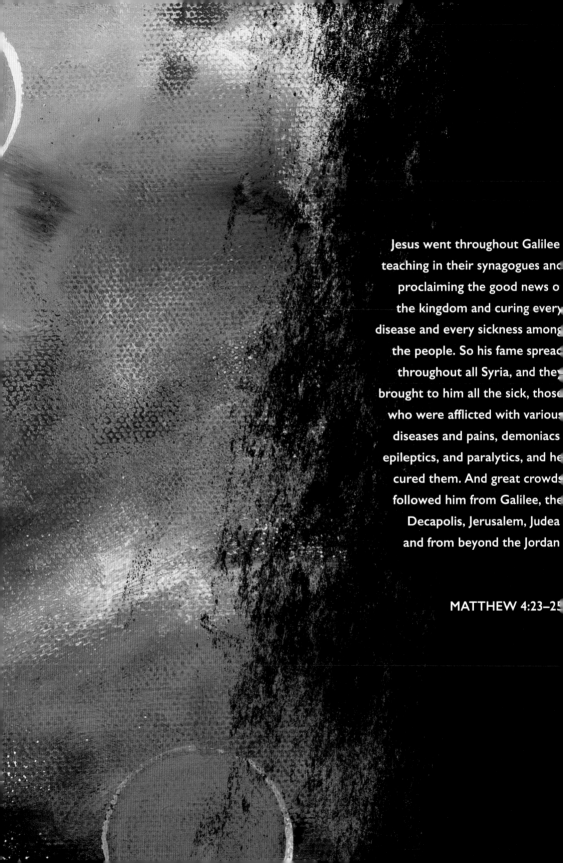

Jesus went throughout Galilee
teaching in their synagogues and
proclaiming the good news of
the kingdom and curing every
disease and every sickness among
the people. So his fame spread
throughout all Syria, and they
brought to him all the sick, those
who were afflicted with various
diseases and pains, demoniacs
epileptics, and paralytics, and he
cured them. And great crowds
followed him from Galilee, the
Decapolis, Jerusalem, Judea
and from beyond the Jordan

MATTHEW 4:23–25

THEN

Jesus,
the teacher,
the healer,
the proclaimer
went throughout Galilee
changing lives.
Demoniacs. Epileptics. Paralytics.
Cured by his healing touch.
Great crowds followed him.
Word began to spread.

NOW

To follow someone means something very different today.

I am fairly active on social media, especially on Facebook and Instagram.
I have tried to use Twitter, but it just doesn't work well for me.

I love sharing photos, funny stories, and inspirational memes
and messages. I love keeping up with friends and family. I love
being connected to church colleagues far and wide.

It's mostly life-giving. Except when it is not.

My teenage daughter often asks me, "How many followers do you have?"

You see ... having lots of followers on social media is important these
days. It is often seen as a way to gauge your popularity or influence. In the
world we live in, popularity and influence are of paramount importance.

It can also be exhausting and lonely.

We are more connected than we ever have been—
and less connected than we ever have been.

Nothing can replace personal contact, face-to-
face connection, and physical touch.

I am an introvert so it takes work for me to be with people—in the
flesh. It is so much easier for me to hide behind an edited photo or silly
post. But I have learned how to do it and my life is so much richer for it.

We read in the Bible that great
crowds followed Jesus.

Following Jesus came with a cost. People left
their families and friends behind. Fishermen
put their nets and occupations away.
Sons and daughters left their parents.

Great crowds followed Jesus and they did so
because Jesus represented so much that they
hungered for . . . things like justice, hope, and love.

Look around you today.

Have the "great crowds that followed
Jesus" diminished in number?

Sometimes I wonder where they are. The
voices seem quiet. Their passion diminished.

Jesus still calls us to follow him—but
he isn't looking for followers just to
ramp up his social media numbers.

Jesus is calling us to be the:
Light in the darkness
The hand that lifts up
The smile that gives hope
The arms that say welcome home
The ears that hear the cries for justice

FOR
REFLECTION

How can you be
Christ in the world?

Where is this need
the greatest?

VI. WHAT SORT OF MAN IS THIS?

And when he got into the boat, his disciples followed him. A windstorm arose on the sea, so great that the boat was being swamped by the waves; but he was asleep. And they went and woke him up, saying, "Lord, save us! We are perishing!" And he said to them, "Why are you afraid, you of little faith?" Then he got up and rebuked the winds and the sea; and there was a dead calm. They were amazed, saying, "What sort of man is this, that even the winds and the sea obey him?"

MATTHEW 8:23–27

THEN

The winds began to blow and the boat began to toss and shudder.

"Maybe it will settle down," they discussed among themselves.

But it did not settle down. It got much worse.

The destructive power of the angry wind increased and the boat began to take on water.

Jesus was weary and had fallen asleep. Even as the storm raged around him, he slept.

The disciples, with great fear and anguish, awoke him.

"Lord, save us! We are perishing!"

As the winds continued to batter the failing boat, Jesus turned to them and asked a question.

"Why?"

"Why are you so afraid?"

"You of little faith."

Jesus then admonished the wind and waves—demanding their stillness.

Then calm.

And amazement.

"What sort of man is this, that even the winds and sea obey him?"

NOW

The storms continue to rage around us.

Turn the TV on. Read the headlines. "Breaking news" flashes across our screens.

Breaking news is just that—crushing, frightening, and infuriating. It breaks our collective hearts and we are weighted down by the hopelessness.

Storms are raging all around us and we fear the boat will sink.

Political storms. Gun violence. Abuse of power. Addiction of all kinds. Violence against women. Violence against children. Violence against lesbian, gay, bisexual, and transgender people. Violence against those who worship differently or look dissimilar than we do.

"Lord, save us! We are perishing!" the disciples cried out.

"Lord, save us! We are perishing!" we cry out.

My reflection, written shortly after the tragic events of September 11, 2001, still holds true today.

When tragedy strikes, we pray that there might be survivors.

Bruised and battered hands reached into the dark hoping to grasp the hand of one of the missing.

We must continue to reach out away from ourselves—into the quagmire of fear and disbelief . . . into that place where there is no hope.

Our hands must reach into that place where there is no place; no place to hang on for dear life . . .

The no place can be a scary place.

In that no place of twisted metal and shattered dreams we do see another hand. It reaches toward us—open, strong, forgiving—pierced.

Reach out—take that hand . . . And hold on . . . for dear life.

FOR REFLECTION

What storms are raging in your life? Is there a time when you experienced Jesus's calming presence in the storm? Describe what that was like.

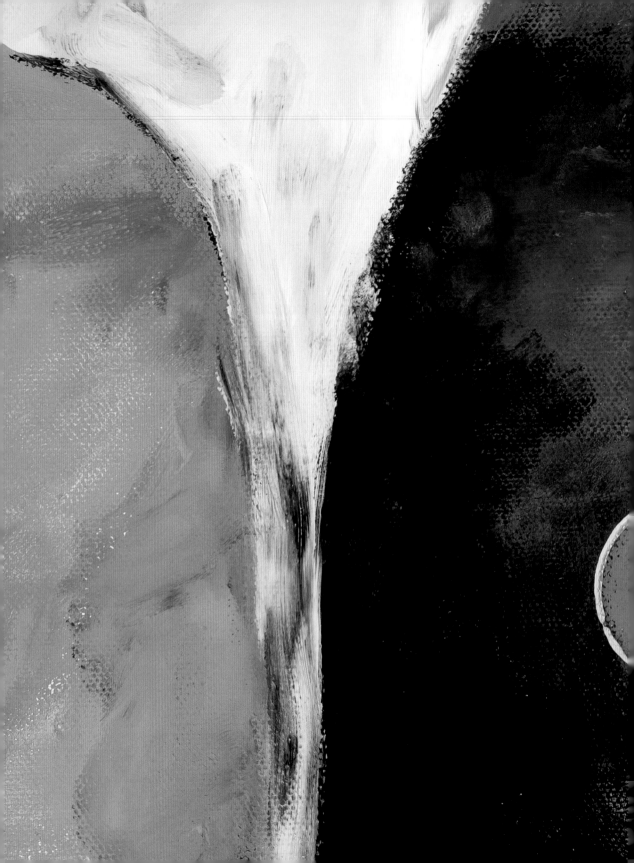

VII. LET ANYONE WITH EARS LISTEN

That same day Jesus went out of the house and sat beside the sea. Such great crowds gathered around him that he got into a boat and sat there, while the whole crowd stood on the beach. And he told them many things in parables, saying: "Listen! A sower went out to sow. And as he sowed, some seeds fell on the path, and the birds came and ate them up. Other seeds fell on rocky ground, where they did not have much soil, and they sprang up quickly, since they had no depth of soil. But when the sun rose, they were scorched; and since they had no root, they withered away. Other seeds fell among thorns, and the thorns grew up and choked them. Other seeds fell on good soil and brought forth grain, some a hundredfold, some sixty, some thirty. Let anyone with ears listen!"

MATTHEW 13:1–9

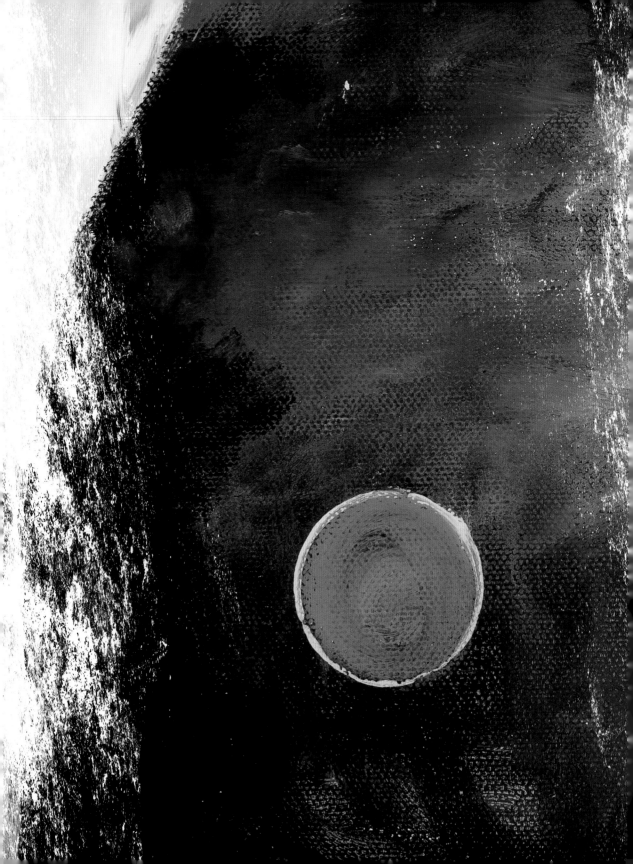

THEN

The crowds that had come to hear Jesus were now so large
that he chose to speak to them from a small boat.

Men, women, and children turned to the man
in the boat as he began to speak.

Jesus loved to tell parables—enigmatic stories
that carried a deeper message.

On this day he told them many parables including one
about a farmer who went out to plant some seeds.

Some of the seed became food for the birds.

Some of the seed fell among the rocks.
It grew quickly but was burned by the sun.

Other seed fell prey to the thorns.

Some of the seed fell on good soil.

From this good soil came a harvest so fruitful
that it produced crop after crop.

Common stories used to teach the crowds
about faith, justice, and love.

"Whoever has ears, let them hear."

NOW

I am a forty-five-year-old man and I struggle with hearing loss.

In fact, I have an incredible pair of hearing aids, but I don't wear them very often. I'm self-centered and much too self-conscious. It's a shame really. Hearing aids are expensive and there are people out there who struggle with hearing loss every day and will never have the opportunity or ability to purchase their own. I'm getting better at wearing them, though. I am grateful that they are small and match my gray hair. (See, that pride thing creeps in.)

I'm a child of the eighties. I had a small transistor radio, but my life changed when I received my first Sony Walkman. Sounds of Michael Jackson and "Thriller" filled my ears and the ears of millions of other children and teens just like me. I loved to "pump up the volume" and I could dance like MC Hammer with the best of them. (Don't ask me to do that now. I have a teenager and she would fall over if I embarrassed her like that.)

When I first went to my audiologist, she told me that she was seeing people with hearing loss like mine at younger and younger ages. My assumption was that this kind of hearing loss affected old people, not someone in their late thirties or early forties.

So, listening has taken on new meaning and urgency for me. I now listen with my ears and my eyes. An important part of listening for me is reading lips. I often miss what is being said when people turn their heads away from me or look down when they are talking. It can be frustrating and isolating.

Jesus was not really talking about hearing loss like mine when he said, "Let anyone with ears listen." Perhaps he was telling us to pay attention to the stories and parables around us. Those stories and parables are still being contemplated today.

We just don't listen very well.

Are you a good listener?

How might you use or
strengthen this skill in
your service to God?

VIII. DO NOT BE AFRAID

Immediately he made the disciples
get into the boat and go on ahead to
the other side, while he dismissed the
crowds. And after he had dismissed the
crowds, he went up the mountain by
himself to pray. When evening came,
he was there alone, but by this time
the boat, battered by the waves, was
far from the land, for the wind was
against them. And early in the morning
he came walking toward them on
the sea. But when the disciples saw
him walking on the sea, they were
terrified, saying, "It is a ghost!" And
they cried out in fear. But immediately
Jesus spoke to them and said, "Take
heart, it is I; do not be afraid."

MATTHEW 14:22–27

THEN

Miracles. Parables. People. So many people.

Jesus was weary and needed
to be alone—so he sent the
crowds on their way.

The disciples had wanted to send
the people away—hungry.

Jesus said "no" and blessed the
bread. "There is plenty," he said.

Jesus blessed the fish.

There was more than enough
food. Twelve baskets full.

He sent them away with full
hearts and full bellies.

Jesus then told his disciples to "go."

"Get on the boat and go
to the other side."

Needing to be alone, Jesus climbed a
mountain and fell to his knees in prayer.

The night was a tumultuous one for the
disciples. Their boat, battered and listless,
was floating aimlessly far from shore.

Then. There he was.

Jesus was walking toward them.

Jesus was walking on the water.

The disciples trembled with fear
for they thought it was a ghost.

"Do not be afraid," he said.

"It is I; do not be afraid."

NOW

When I was a child, my best friend was from Cambodia.
He had escaped to the United States in the 1980s
by boat. I have often wondered what that boat
trip must have been like. He never spoke of it.

We spent our childhood fishing together—brothers
from different worlds, but brothers just the same.

He died when we were in our early twenties from a
very aggressive form of brain cancer. My heart was
not just broken when he died. It was shattered. I was
filled with anger, fear, and such sadness. He was here
for such a short time—yet he taught me so much.

I went to the water alone, and fished, and cried, and prayed.

As recent as this morning, I went down to the
water to fish, to pray, and to be with my friend.

I see him in the sparkling water. I sense his presence
in the thrill of catching a fish. He is with me. Always.

"Do not be afraid." I hear his voice on the wind.

"It is I; do not be afraid."

FOR REFLECTION

What are you
most afraid of?

Do you think Jesus
ever felt fear?

IX. A BRIGHT CLOUD OVERSHADOWED THEM

Six days later, Jesus took with him
Peter and James and his brother
John and led them up a high
mountain, by themselves. And he
was transfigured before them,
and his face shone like the sun,
and his clothes became dazzling
white. Suddenly there appeared
to them Moses and Elijah, talking
with him. Then Peter said to
Jesus, "Lord, it is good for us to
be here; if you wish, I will make
three dwellings here, one for
you, one for Moses, and one
for Elijah." While he was still
speaking, suddenly a bright cloud
overshadowed them, and from
the cloud a voice said, "This
is my Son, the Beloved; with
him I am well pleased; listen to
him!" When the disciples heard
this, they fell to the ground and
were overcome by fear. But Jesus
came and touched them, saying,
"Get up and do not be afraid." And
when they looked up, they saw no
one except Jesus himself alone.

MATTHEW 17:1–8

THEN

"How curious!" they wondered
to themselves as they embarked
on this new journey with Jesus.

Jesus quietly led Peter, James, and his
brother John up a high mountain.

It was just the four of them.

Then ... something incredible happened.

Jesus was transfigured before them.

His face radiated like the sun and his
clothing became as white as the light.

They were not the only ones there.

Moses and Elijah appeared and
they were talking with Jesus.

"Let me put up three shelters—one
for you, one for Moses, and one
for Elijah," Peter said to Jesus.

This profound and powerful
experience continued to unfold
when a bright cloud fell over them
and they heard a voice call out.

"Listen to him."

"My son whom I love."

The disciples fell to their faces in fear.

Jesus touched them and said ...

"Get up."

"Do not be afraid."

When they opened their eyes, they
saw Jesus, and no one else.

NOW

It was early morning when I decided
to get out of the bed and go for
a walk down to the ocean.

Sleep had been hard to come by that
night. As it often is, my mind was full
and racing. It was at a time in my life
where I was facing some tough decisions
both in my personal and professional
life, and I thought that the fresh ocean
air would help clear my head.

The salt-tinged morning air was filled
with the sounds of excited seagulls—
like children on a playground. Blurs of
white and gray, darting this way and
that, telling stories that grow more
fantastical with each splash of the waves.

I gazed out across the expanse of the
ocean and set my eyes toward the
horizon. I have always been intrigued
by horizons—the place where the sky
meets the earth. As a child, I would often
draw a thin line of sky at the top of the
paper—a round sun in the top corner.

We often say the sky is "up there," when
really the sky surrounds us and is inside
of us. We breathe it in and lungs are filled.

We often say Jesus is "up there," when
really Jesus surrounds us and is inside of
us. We breathe his breath and our lungs
are filled.

I continued to soak in the beauty of the
early morning light when I saw some
unusual movement in the distance.

It was a small tree, maybe six feet tall,
and it looked like it was on fire. I saw
flashes of orange and yellow and it was
engulfed in what I thought were flames.

I ran down the boardwalk toward the
burning tree. Then I stopped—frozen in
my tracks.

The tree was not on fire. It was engulfed,
though, with hundreds—maybe thousands
—of monarch butterflies, their wings
dancing to the ancient rhythm of creation.

I stood there and wept with joy.

The sky came down
and touched the earth.

I was standing in the
presence of Jesus,
God among us.

"This is my Son, whom I
love; with him I am well
pleased. Listen to him!"

FOR
REFLECTION

Have you ever heard
the voice of God?

Is there a place where
that voice is most clear?

X. LEAVE HER ALONE

Six days before the Passover Jesus came to Bethany, the home of Lazarus, whom he had raised from the dead. There they gave a dinner for him. Martha served, and Lazarus was one of those at the table with him. Mary took a pound of costly perfume made of pure nard, anointed Jesus' feet, and wiped them with her hair. The house was filled with the fragrance of the perfume. But Judas Iscariot, one of his disciples (the one who was about to betray him), said, "Why was this perfume not sold for three hundred denarii and the money given to the poor?" (He said this not because he cared about the poor, but because he was a thief; he kept the common purse and used to steal what was put into it.) Jesus said, "Leave her alone. She bought it so that she might keep it for the day of my burial. You always have the poor with you, but you do not always have me."

JOHN 12:1–8

THEN

Jesus had raised their brother from the dead; Mary and Martha wanted to do something to thank him.

They asked him to come for dinner.

Martha prepared the plates and served the meal to Jesus and their brother, Lazarus.

Mary knelt at Jesus's feet and anointed them with a luxurious and sweet-smelling perfume.

She then wiped his feet with her hair.

The fragrance was intoxicating.

Judas Iscariot, one of Jesus's disciples, was infuriated by this gesture and angrily questioned Jesus.

Judas, with his very dark heart, wanted the money that would have been made if the perfume had been sold—not to give away to the poor, but to line his own purse.

Jesus, knowing what was happening, reprimanded Judas.

"Leave her alone." He was not pleased with Judas's outburst.

"She bought this for the day of my burial."

"You always have the poor with you, but you do not always have me."

NOW

Wheelchairs and recliners circled the room. Some of the residents were asleep; others were singing. Most of them seemed agitated and afraid.

Our youth group had been invited to visit with the residents in the Alzheimer's unit in our local Episcopal retirement community. We attempted to explain to the young people what they might see or hear—that it was okay to feel anxious and ask questions about something they saw or experienced. At first the youth hung close to us—not sure what to do or say. We were told that the residents loved having their hands rubbed with lotion, so we began to ask if anyone wanted us to do that for them.

One of the young women in our group noticed that the lady she was working with kept touching the girl's fingernails and smiling. Her fingernails were covered in a sky blue polish—the same color as the woman's clouding eyes. She ran over to us and told us that she thought the woman wanted her nails painted; could she paint her nails? The nurses gave her permission to do so.

Gently, the young girl took the woman's hand and painted her nails. The woman—who had been very anxious at the beginning of our visit—began to settle down and even started to hum a tune; we think it was a lullaby. Soft and smooth hands held

deeply wrinkled hands, and a deep connection began to form.

I stepped back and looked at the room. Every young person was paired with a resident.

Hands were being massaged. Fingernails were being painted. Smiles were being shared.

Lives were being changed.

It was holy touch.

"Mary took a pound of costly perfume made of pure nard, anointed Jesus's feet and wiped them with her hair. The house was filled with the fragrance of the perfume."

FOR REFLECTION

With whom do you most identify: Mary, Martha, or Judas?

XI. SITTING ON A DONKEY'S COLT

The next day the great crowd that had
come to the festival heard that Jesus
was coming to Jerusalem. So they took
branches of palm trees and went out to
meet him, shouting, "Hosanna! Blessed
is the one who comes in the name of
the Lord—the King of Israel!" Jesus
found a young donkey and sat on it;
as it is written: "Do not be afraid,
daughter of Zion. Look, your king is
coming, sitting on a donkey's colt!"

JOHN 12:12–15

THEN

Word began to spread.

Excited whispers and anticipation electrified the crowd.

The joy was palpable.

Jesus was coming to Jerusalem!

They ran to meet him, covering the dirt path
with discarded cloaks and colorful blankets.

Taking branches of palm trees, they began to shout.

"Hosanna!   Hosanna!   Hosanna!"

"Blessed is the one who comes in the name
of the Lord, the King of Israel!"

Do not be afraid!

The king is coming,

"sitting on a donkey's colt!"

Love has arrived.

"Hosanna!"

NOW

I will never forget him.

When I first visited, he was curled under a blanket in his room—his hospital
room. He had been very sick to his stomach but was now sound asleep.

I could see the shape of his body under the blanket. He was so thin and pale.

After a brief visit with his grandmother, we gathered around
his bed, laid our hands on him, and said a prayer.

There were tears—from all of us.

Weeks passed and as he did time and again, this amazing young man rallied.

He was soon to celebrate his twelfth birthday and wanted to throw a big party.

We knew we had to be there.

Having become quite the celebrity, the hospital commons room was filled with
family and friends who wanted to celebrate this special day with him. There were
balloons, cake, gifts. I couldn't help but notice the other children with bald heads.
Drawn together by a cancer diagnosis, these families hold on to each other for
support and encouragement. Today they had gathered to celebrate his birthday.

He loved these other children and they loved him. He was—and is—their hero.

Although a mask covered his face, you couldn't miss his sparkling eyes.
He was taking it all in and it was obvious that he was having a good time.

Still weak from the battle raging inside of him, he
was seated behind a table—two friends seated
beside him. Guests were invited to step up to
the table to wish him a Happy Birthday.

It was my turn to say hello. His smile and kind
heart were evident, even beneath his mask.

I was there to give him a birthday blessing—
but he was the one who blessed me.

He reached into a box and said, "I have something for you."

It was a small wooden cross.

It was his idea to give everyone in the
room a small wooden cross!

Why? It seemed such a serious and mature gift,
especially for a twelve-year-old's birthday party.

Yet, it was the perfect gift.

This beautiful boy loved Jesus with his whole
heart. His birthday wish was to share that
love with everyone in the room.

**Mahlon Paul Hardt, age 12, boy scout, LEGO™ master,
gamer extraordinaire, loving, laughing boy, died
from Acute Myeloid Leukemia on January 3, 2017.**

FOR
REFLECTION

How do you
welcome Christ?

XII. GO INTO THE CITY

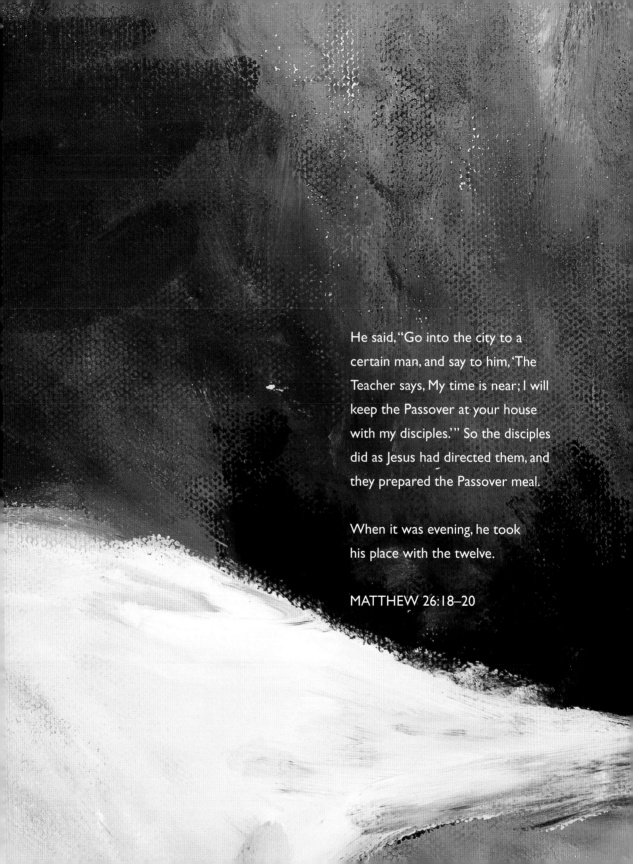

He said, "Go into the city to a certain man, and say to him, 'The Teacher says, My time is near; I will keep the Passover at your house with my disciples.'" So the disciples did as Jesus had directed them, and they prepared the Passover meal.

When it was evening, he took his place with the twelve.

MATTHEW 26:18–20

THEN

"Go into the city," the Teacher
says to his disciples.

Go into the city.

A certain man will receive you.

Tell him.

My time is near.

Let me keep the Passover with
my disciples in your home.

Yes, Jesus. We will do this for you.

They prepared the meal
for their Teacher.

Inside.

Their hearts were breaking.

NOW

With a population of 2.1 million and growing, Houston, Texas, is currently the fourth largest and most diverse city in the United States and is on track to become the third largest city in just a few short years.

It was never a place I imagined living.

We moved to the big city in June of 2015.

Two years later, we are still here. I own a pair of cowboy boots and we bought a house. I guess we are going to be here a while.

We certainly did not know what to think when we arrived. Houston is a huge place. The traffic is indescribable, the food is spectacular, and the humidity is stifling.

We had been here for less than a week when we received two invitations—one to a Houston Astros baseball game and the other to a meal at one of our local Turkish Muslim centers. If that doesn't sum up Houston in a sentence, nothing can.

The baseball game was our first experience of a Texas-sized sporting event and it was awesome. It was "Episcopal Night at the Astros," so there were lots of Episcopalians gathered in one place. Everyone was friendly and welcoming. Even with our moving boxes still needing to be unpacked, Kristin and I were already beginning to feel like this was a place we could call home.

The following week, parishioners from the church I serve were invited to join a local Turkish Muslim community for an Iftar dinner, a special nightly meal during the season of Ramadan. It was an evening of friendship, prayer, community, food, and joy.

Seated around the tables were Christians and Muslims gathered in community, learning from each other, and realizing that we are more alike than we are different.

With prayers from the Koran and prayers from the Book of Common Prayer, the meal was blessed and bread was broken. God was no doubt in the midst of this holy gathering.

Kristin and I became fast friends with the family we shared our meal with. Mehmet and his children have touched our lives over these past two years in countless ways. On Thanksgiving, Mehmet texted me to let me know he gives thanks for our friendship. One evening, he shared with us the meaningful ritual of preparing and partaking in the experience of Turkish coffee. He even prepared for us a treat of "Noah's Pudding." In Turkey, Noah's Pudding is a traditional dish that symbolizes the celebratory meal Noah made when he came off the ark. It is a sign of peace, of community, and of a bright future.

We live in a world where fear of the "other" threatens to take hold.

We can't let that happen.

My deepest prayer is that we continue to gather around the table—human beings made in the image of God—and share with each other the holy bread of peace and love.

Moving to the big city was scary for each one of us. Our families were a thousand miles away and we were moving to a land we did not know. Yet we opened ourselves to new possibilities, a new call. This big city is now our home. Our families are still a thousand miles away—but they are also here, gathered in peace around the table.

FOR REFLECTION

Have you ever experienced community over
the act of sharing a meal? What was that like?

XIII. YOU CANNOT COME

"Little children, I am with you only a little longer. You will look for me; and as I said to the Jews so now I say to you, 'Where I am going, you cannot come.' I give you a new commandment, that you love one another. Just as I have loved you, you also should love one another. By this everyone will know that you are my disciples, if you have love for one another."

JOHN 13:33–35

THEN

The light from the oil lantern's curling flame flickered across their wearied faces.

With rapt attention they listened to their Teacher.

"Little children, I am with you only a little longer."

Jesus's eyes sparkled and shined in the dancing light.

"Please don't look for me."

"You will not find me."

"Where I am going, you cannot come."

Silence, like a pall, fell about them.

Now listen closely to me.

Love one another.

I command you.

Love one another—just as I have loved you.

Do this and everyone will know that you are mine.

I love you.

NOW

They found her on the floor in her kitchen.

When she didn't show up for church that morning, they knew something was wrong.

She had taken a pan of corn bread out of the oven and sat it on the stove to cool. As it had for so many years, the smell of the sweet bread filled the kitchen.

She walked down to the mailbox and returned to the kitchen, where she began to open her mail.

They found her the next day. It was a stroke—immediate and massive.

I was summoned to come and see her in the hospital.

It was a long drive from North Carolina to the little hospital in Louisiana.

Her grandchildren gathered around her; we held her hand and told her how much we loved her. The stroke had changed her face and rendered her unable to speak, but her eyes still sparkled and I knew she knew I was there.

She wanted to go home to die.

I was at her home when the ambulance arrived. It was a beautiful day. The birds were singing, the yellow bells in her garden were in full bloom, and her home was filled with those who loved her most.

She was moved to her bedroom where she could see her beloved Louisiana sky; she was covered with one of her own homemade quilts.

Within a few short days, she was gone. She was finally with her Creator. Her entire life had been focused on being with the one who gave her breath. She was now home.

She was and will always be an important part of my life. Her kitchen table became my painting table. Her handmade quilts still cover and comfort us as we fall asleep each night. Memories of our fishing trips bring me such laughter and joy.

Her greatest gift to me was teaching me how to love, in the truest sense of the word.

"I give you a new commandment, that you love one another. Just as I have loved you, you also should love one another. By this everyone will know that you are my disciples, if you have love for one another."

FOR REFLECTION

What do you think Jesus means when he says, "Love one another"?

XIV. YOU WILL BE WITH ME IN PARADISE

One of the criminals who were hanged there kept deriding him and saying, "Are you not the Messiah? Save yourself and us!" But the other rebuked him, saying, "Do you not fear God, since you are under the same sentence of condemnation? And we indeed have been condemned justly, for we are getting what we deserve for our deeds, but this man has done nothing wrong." Then he said, "Jesus, remember me when you come into your kingdom." He replied, "Truly I tell you, today you will be with me in Paradise."

LUKE 23:39–43

THEN

Criminals.

Nailed to the cross.

Guilty as charged.

And Jesus.

"Save yourself!" shouted the criminal.

"Are you not the Messiah?"

The weight of their bodies brought excruciating pain.

"Stop it!" shouted the other criminal.

Sweat and blood on furrowed brow.

"We are guilty!"

"This man has done nothing wrong."

With failing breath and racing heart, the criminal turned his head to Jesus.

"Remember me."

"Remember. Me."

"Remember."

"Me."

Jesus heard the man's pleading voice and said,

"You will

be with me

in Paradise."

"Today."

NOW

The memory of a story from many years ago . . .

She has found her voice. Riley is almost two years old and has already drawn some pretty amazing conclusions about what the big world is all about.

Mornings in the Hutchison house are special. They begin quite early—most mornings we are up at 5:00 a.m. Kristin teaches school and I like getting to work when the halls are quiet and the phones are not yet awake. The best time of the morning is at 6:00 a.m. when I open Riley's bedroom door. There is a brief rustling of "Bear" (she calls him "Beer"), her "bankey," and her "pappies." Her head pops up and she says, "Cuddle with Daddy." We cuddle on the couch and drink "coffee" together. She has warm milk with a little flavored creamer in it, and I have the real stuff. I adore this time of the morning.

One recent Wednesday morning, as we were getting ready to get in the car to head to a working breakfast, Riley looked up at the star-filled morning sky and said, "Hi, Aggie!"

It was the sweetest sound. Aggie, my wife's beloved childhood pet, had died a few weeks before. Aggie was special to all of us—especially Riley. I was surprised with her comment, so I asked her to tell me where Aggie was.

"Daddy, Aggie is in the
stars with the angels."

In her pure voice with a smile on her face,
she was letting us know that Aggie was
fine. Aggie was in the stars with the angels.
I looked up at the sky, and with Riley's
voice still echoing in my ears, I saw the
faces of friends, family members, and yes,
even pets that I thought were gone. They
are not gone. Uttered by the small child
with bright eyes and an innocent heart—
they are in the stars with the angels.

Riley looked up at me this morning
while we were cuddling.
I had a smile on my face and
she said, "Daddy happy."

Yes, baby. Daddy is very happy.

"Truly I tell you, today you will
be with me in paradise."

FOR REFLECTION

Who do you most identify with
in the Bible story? Why?

XV. HE BREATHED HIS LAST

It was now about noon, and darkness came over the whole land until three in the afternoon, while the sun's light failed; and the curtain of the temple was torn in two. Then Jesus, crying with a loud voice, said, "Father, into your hands I commend my spirit." Having said this, he breathed his last. When the centurion saw what had taken place, he praised God and said, "Certainly this man was innocent." And when all the crowds who had gathered there for this spectacle saw what had taken place, they returned home, beating their breasts. But all his acquaintances, including the women who had followed him from Galilee, stood at a distance, watching these things.

Now there was a good and righteous man named Joseph, who, though a member of the council, had not agreed to their plan and action. He came from the Jewish town of Arimathea, and he was waiting expectantly for the kingdom of God. This man went to Pilate and asked for the body of Jesus. Then he took it down, wrapped it in a linen cloth, and laid it in a rock-hewn tomb where no one had ever been laid. It was the day of Preparation, and the sabbath was beginning. The women who had come with him from Galilee followed, and they saw the tomb and how his body was laid. Then they returned, and prepared spices and ointments.

On the sabbath they rested according to the commandment.

LUKE 23:44–56

THEN

The Light.

Eclipsed by Darkness.

The curtain of the temple

Torn.

"Into your hands!

I commend my spirit!"

Jesus takes his last breath.

NOW

I am a bird lover. I
always have been.

It was midmorning and we
were in the middle of a staff
meeting. As I sometimes
do, I was staring out of the
window, not really paying
attention, when all of the
sudden I saw a bird fly into
one of the office windows.
Her body fell to the ground.
She was still moving, so
I thought; with time, she
was going to make it.

Later that day, around three
in the afternoon, I walked out
of my office and saw a group
of my colleagues gathered
around a cardboard box. One
of them had found the bird
and put her in the box. She
was still alive and they were
trying to decide what to do.

I looked down at her and knew in my heart and soul what needed to happen. It appeared that she had a broken neck and was getting weaker by the moment. The only way she was ever going to fly again would be when her spirit was set free from her earthly body.

I looked at my colleagues who were obviously heartbroken. Even though birds flying into windows are an all-too-common occurrence, this group of people was grieving and they seemed to be looking at me for the answer.

"She's not going to make it," I said.

My throat felt like it was filled with cotton. She was suffering, so I knew that I could not let her lie there until she died. I knew I had to end her misery.

After she was set free from her shattered body, I looked closely at her. I had never seen a bird like her before. Her beak was a bright yellow. Her body a soft white and tan. Bold white spots covered her tail's underside. She was spectacular. I found out later that she was a yellow-billed cuckoo.

I dug a hole, said a prayer, thanked her for her song, and gently buried her in the flower bed.

I still think about her when I pass that flower bed or hear her song on the wind.

"It was now about noon, and darkness came over the whole land until three in the afternoon, while the sun's light failed; and the curtain of the temple was torn in two. Then Jesus, crying with a loud voice, said, 'Father, into your hands I commend my spirit.' Having said this, he breathed his last."

FOR REFLECTION

Close your eyes and focus intently on your breath. Listen to the sounds as it enters and departs your body. Don't rush. Take your time. Breathe deeply––in and out. Breathe through your nose and let it fill your lungs. Hold it there. Breathe out through your mouth fervently praying for the one who gives you breath.

XVI. PEACE BE WITH YOU

When he was at the table with them, he took bread, blessed and broke it, and gave it to them. Then their eyes were opened, and they recognized him; and he vanished from their sight. They said to each other, "Were not our hearts burning within us while he was talking to us on the road, while he was opening the scriptures to us?" That same hour they got up and returned to Jerusalem; and they found the eleven and their companions gathered together. They were saying, "The Lord has risen indeed, and he has appeared to Simon!" Then they told what had happened on the road, and how he had been made known to them in the breaking of the bread.

While they were talking about this, Jesus himself stood among them and said to them, "Peace be with you." They were startled and terrified, and thought that they were seeing a ghost. He said to them, "Why are you frightened, and why do doubts arise in your hearts? Look at my hands and my feet; see that it is I myself. Touch me and see; for a ghost does not have flesh and bones as you see that I have." And when he had said this, he showed them his hands and his feet. While in their joy they were disbelieving and still wondering, he said to them, "Have you anything here to eat?"

They gave him a piece of broiled fish, and he took it and ate in their presence.

Then he said to them, "These are my words that I spoke to you while I was still with you—that everything written about me in the law of Moses, the prophets, and the psalms must be fulfilled." Then he opened their minds to understand the scriptures, and he said to them, "Thus it is written, that the Messiah is to suffer and to rise from the dead on the third day, and that repentance and forgiveness of sins is to be proclaimed in his name to all nations, beginning from Jerusalem. You are witnesses of these things. And see, I am sending upon you what my Father promised; so stay here in the city until you have been clothed with power from on high."

Then he led them out as far as Bethany, and, lifting up his hands, he blessed them. While he was blessing them, he withdrew from them and was carried up into heaven. And they worshiped him, and returned to Jerusalem with great joy; and they were continually in the temple blessing God.

—LUKE 24:30–53

THEN

Early in the morning
before the sun had
broached the horizon,
women
with spices prepared
for the body
went to the tomb.
They made their way
toward the tomb.
The stone.
Rolled away.
No body!
How peculiar!

Suddenly
two men in dazzling
clothes appeared
and stood beside the two
women.

Terrified.
The women turned
their faces away.

"Why do you look for
the living among the dead?"
"He is not here."
"He is alive!"

N O W

"Hey, Mr. Roger!"

"What's up, Mr. Roger?"

I hear greetings like these every day.
We have a high school that is located
on the church property where I serve.
My office is just down the hallway from
their offices so the students are always
sticking their heads in and saying hello.

Normally, a simple story like this
one wouldn't mean very much. But
this is not a normal story.

The school these students attend is the
largest sober high school in the nation. This
special high school supports the educational
needs of teens in recovery. These students are
offered an opportunity to grow (academically,
emotionally, socially, and spiritually) by
integrating the principles of recovery into daily
education. They strive to create a community
of diversity, compassion, and mutual respect.

They look like students at any other high
school. They look and sound like my own
teenage daughter. Yet, these students are
different—different in the sense that they
are fighting a life and death battle every day.

Many of them—if not all of them—have
looked death in the face. For some of them,
death comes out on the winning side.
But most of the time death is vanquished. The
young people want to live ... And they do.

Early in my time here, I was sitting at my desk
when I heard a knock on my door. What
I saw caught me off guard. A student was
standing in my doorway holding a bright pink
gerbera daisy. "I wanted to give this to you,"
he said with a smile. "I am glad you are here."
I later learned that these students often go
out into the community—specifically the
nearby Texas Medical Center—and give
these flowers or some other symbol of
kindness to people on the street—homeless
people, medical center staff, patients,
security personnel, and more. I happened
to be one of the recipients that day.

I've always been told that you shouldn't say
"I love you" unless you really mean it. I have
now learned that we should say it more.
Every day the students are here, I hear the
words "I love you!" ring through the hallways.
The teachers, staff, and administrators say
those words to every student—all day long.
The students reciprocate; or are the first
ones to say it. I never experienced this
in school; I don't think it was allowed.
When I asked about this, the staff shared

with me that these young people need
to know that they are loved—no matter
what. Sometimes that love comes in the
shape of those three words. Sometimes
that love comes in the form of increased
boundaries or suspension. Sometimes
that love comes in the form of a call to
the authorities or a trip to the hospital.
Sometimes love means letting them go,
not knowing what the outcome will be.

Each month, I have the opportunity
of sharing the Painting Table with the
students. Recently, I asked them to create
an artistic representation of where they
saw their lives at this moment in time.
One of the young women began to paint
a tree. The left side of the tree was dead.
The limbs were dark, fragile, and bare.
Then she began to paint the other side of
the tree. The branches, extending out from
the same trunk, were strong, expansive,
and covered with bright green leaves. This
side of the tree was very much alive.
Her roots and branches were growing
stronger. The dead branches would always
be a part of her, but the love, nourishment,
and support she was receiving gave her life.

FOR REFLECTION

The young woman drew a picture
of a tree with dead and living
branches. How might you reflect
your life in words and images?

AFTERWORD

I don't often remember my dreams.

This time I did.

It was a totem pole—but it featured people, not animals.

I saw a baby, a young boy, a man, and . . .

Could it be?

Yes. It was.

It was the crucified Christ.

The totem pole in my dreams was of the life of Jesus—from infant born
in a manger to the crucified Christ with his arms stretched wide.

I awoke with a start and was distracted by my dream the rest of the day.

I knew I had to paint a picture of it.

So I did.

This book features different segments of the painting. The
concluding image of the book is the painting in its entirety.

My favorite part of the painting is Jesus's arms. They run off
of the side of the canvas and continue into infinity.

That is love, people.

Arms stretched wide to receive all.

Maybe it was what I had for dinner combined with this Texas heat.

It was vivid and real.

A thin-place moment I will never forget.

Or maybe it was the words of the Most Reverend Michael B. Curry,
the XXVII Presiding Bishop of the Episcopal Church. His social media
presence (and of course his preaching) is masterful, and his "This is the
Jesus Movement" video clip moves me to tears every time I watch it.

He's walking through the city as the world moves around him.

He speaks of Jesus. Love. The Gospel.

A baby cries.

I am so glad that part was not edited out of the video.

A baby cries.

Jesus: God among us

Peace to you.

"Now is our time to go. To go into the world to share the good news of God and Jesus Christ. To go into the world and help to be agents and instruments of God's reconciliation. To go into the world, let the world know that there is a God who loves us, a God who will not let us go, and that that love can set us all free."

The Most Reverend Michael Bruce Curry
XXVII Presiding Bishop and Primate of the Episcopal Church